Will It Ever Go Away?

Will It Ever Go Away?

thoughts and poetry authored by
Ciara Mason

*thank you to the man who shattered my soul
and to the people who have supported me
through my life's journey,
i would not be where i am today
without you.*

PART ONE

my dad's gone crazy.

we need to talk,
your dad is dead.

when your father commits suicide,
your life becomes
a before and after.

she spoke about him in the past tense,
my mother said he loved us very much.
that's when i knew he was dead.

my heart is pounding loudly in my chest.
my anxiety devours me from the inside out.
my mouth is as dry as a bone.

i succumb to paralysis.

the shock of horror,
the rush of relief,
the cascade of pain.

"he was a very disturbed man"
they had said to me.

how could i ever imagine my father like that?

the light dimmed down to a gloomy hue
the day you left the earth.
the colours don't shine as boldly
as they once did.

the hospital refused his entry.
his sister refused to call for help.
my father refused his own life.

i refuse to accept my new reality.

they said things would have been different
if he had seen his children.

but is it true?

because he was watching us the whole time.

why is everyone ignoring me?
it seems to me
that everyone is afraid
of death.

old enough to understand,
not wise enough to know why.

when he died
i stared at the wall.

when he died
there was nothing of his to hold.

when he died
the sun still rose.

when he died
a piece of me died too.

where does the soul find its home?

the void he left behind,
i am drowning in.
please come back and save me.

grief is so much more
than just being sad.

i yearn for what no longer exists.

it is so terrifying and so intense,
that my gut drops to the bottom of the earth,
with the realisation that you are never
coming home.

i may be numb
but i will not numb myself.
not like you did.

how do i navigate this?

i don't believe this will ever end.

a government statistic,
that is what my father has become.

the gas you cannot inhale,
the drugs that transport you,
the vices you share with others,
the soul you chose to never uncover.

i'm so highly emotional,
now i'm crying for no reason.
they think i'm weird and unstable.

like a branch in the wind,
you are unpredictable.

tunnel vision.

grief-stricken.
that i am.
we will all experience
at least once,
maybe more.

dead father jokes,
my coping mechanism.

if he loved me,

why did my dad commit suicide?

death.
i hate you.
you bring everyone so much pain.

be that as it may,
no one can escape you.

did he think of his children
before he took his last breath?

how am i to feel
when i hear "good riddance"
regarding the death of my father.

my counsellor told me
to forget the bad memories,
but now,
all i can think of are the good.
it is killing me slowly.

i want to be reunited with my father.
but not wanting to kill myself
keeps me separate
from him.

i had no idea.
i was just a child,
i don't know much about you.

where were my flowers?

why did you bring me into this world
if you weren't going to be there for me?

i cannot protect my dad from himself.
i am only his daughter.

just what we need
for this family of three.

i think i saw you in my sleep,
but you don't visit me enough.

i need someone to hold me,
piece me back together
because i am falling apart.

where are you?

my body is numb,
i cannot feel.

though my hands shake,
is this real?
i am stunned,
i have no feeling.
that man should not
have been leaving.
let me cry, let me cry.
my own father has taken his life.
i wail and heave
and i cannot breathe.

i cannot feel,
my body is numb.

are you happier now?

taken away to the dark side,
never to return to the light.

falling into the void
that you may be.

i don't want to let go.
i don't want to be free.

everyone i love is going to die,
and so will i.

i think about this before i sleep,
ever since i was four.

you hugged me.
you told me you loved me,
that you were going to miss me
and that you were sorry.
over
and over
and over.

i was confused.

i did not realise that you knew
it would be our last goodbye.

tell humans you love them.

i cannot comprehend.
i won't allow myself.
in my mind, you're still alive.
i'm not in denial.
i know i will see you again one day.
maybe you'll come to my front door,
and i'll faint from pure joy to know
that you are still here.

i cannot remember his mannerisms and that
worries me.

he hung himself high
or maybe he hung himself low.

in a motel room
or was it a hotel room?

i'm not sure.

i am sure that the hospital
could not spare him a bed.

they should not have left him alone.

losing the beat of my heart
due to these deep wounded scars.

will i be punished?
will i pay for all my father's sins?

you abandoned me,
how can i forgive you?

you broke our soul contract,
how can i forgive you?

you are meant to protect me,
how can i forgive you?

you still had so much to teach me,
how can i forgive you?

i'm your daughter and you're my dad,
how can i forgive you?

i died in that house
when we all left each other.
i've never been the same.

will i spend eternity
searching for you?

crows are the souls of the suicide.

you'll never find the girl
that once existed
before this
again.

i lost my innocence,
it wasn't intended.

how come i've forgotten how to be happy?

would you still do it?
would you still do it if you knew?
if you knew how devastated,
how devastated i would be?

i don't know what to do.

nothing could've prepared me for this.

no thought in my mind,
no doubt in my bones,
no hate in my heart.

please visit me in my dreams
and stay a while longer.

if at first, you don't succeed,
you try again
and again.
again,
and again.
a few more times now.
then again, again, and again.

until you succeed.

i assume he's still alive,
just in hiding
and he'll come by one day,

just to surprise me.

why
did
no
one
care?

how was i to know
that this would be my life.

i don't know where you are.

how do i find you?

and in these small moments
when i catch a glimpse
of a father and daughter,
all i want is for him to be alive.

i guess
there was just something wrong inside.

as i take a sip from my cuppa tea,
i remember how you used to make these for me.
a dash of milk and three sugars, please.

he really did love me.

i question my sanity for i am half of you.
my blood encompasses all your trauma,
don't let me drown in it.

god, save his soul.
may the angels guide him back to safety.

i love photos,
i love visual memories.

that's how i know i didn't make it up.

Thoughts on my 25th birthday

i have now lived longer than i have known my
dad.
this makes me feel very uneasy.
i see you holding me, smiling at me and being
with me,
but i am no longer that young girl.
i have lived many years without you
and will continue to do so.
this frightens me to the core.

what happens on earth,
stays on earth.

it is difficult for me to understand.

you had everything
and chose to have nothing.

come back, please.
i beg you.
i see you in everything.

you're still earthbound right?

my grief is my issue,
not yours.

happiness surrounds me,
but it is not mine to keep.

i need to heal, i need to grieve.
these seven stages are real,
however,
they are not linear.

tonight's the night,
my debutante ball.
it's the special father-daughter dance.
i scan the floor
trying to locate you,
but you're nowhere to be found.

a little girl.

she is
confused.

she is
crushed.

she is
heartbroken.

she is
my inner child.

my children,
my partners,
my friends,
my colleagues,
my peers,

even strangers,

will never know you.

it was a sunny, clear, blue sky day,
minutes pass and the clouds roll in.
a storm starts to brew,
it hangs for a while.
it grows stronger with time,
consuming everything in its path.
the gusts of winds are rough,
the rain pelts down like needles.
stinging and burning the skin.
you begin to pray for the blue skies to come
back
but you've collapsed into this lust.
it is addicting and you don't want to leave.
the thunder roars
after the blinding lightning
strikes your body.
again,
and again.
it's riveting, it's dangerous, it's confusing,
you're lost.
the hail assaults the earth,
it's bone-chilling.
yet the cheap excitement engrosses you.

now,
that the storm has passed,
you find yourself all alone

and there is no way out.

a girl's first heartbreak
is meant to be some stupid boy,

not her father.

his life had a tragic ending,
one that could have been avoided.

it could have been avoided.

it did not need to happen.

it could have been avoided.

fuck this.

my dad no longer exists on this earth,
still, he continues to exist on my face.

grief has heightened my fear of loss and
abandonment.

i will not leave people
in fear of making them feel
the same way i did
on the seventeenth of july 2015.

hope, it's dangerous.

it haunts me,

as i hope for the impossible.

fractured memories
stare back at me
from all the photographs
i choose to keep.

my chest is empty and hollow.
i can't breathe properly.

hey god,
we need to talk.

i miss you so much my heart hurts
and i struggle to draw breath.

i'm soaking tissues
and scream crying until i retch.

my previous life feels like a hallucination.

my brother and i
were the last ones to know
about his death.

he died two days before we were told.

ignorance is bliss.

unconditional love
was stolen from me.

i still don't know where you are.

suicide doesn't end the pain,
it just passes it onto someone else.

i guess i must accept the truth.

my eyes are tired,
my head is empty,
my body is sore,
my heart is broken,
my soul is frozen.

wreathed in smiles
when you're around
in the atmosphere.

my dad is becoming a stranger.

how do i truly know that you're no longer?
if i haven't seen your dead body.

i pray and hope that everyone is lying to me,
that this is a long-lasting joke and you'll come to
see me.

but when i see you in my dream
and you don't say a word.

my heart unwillingly accepts
that you no longer roam this earth.

i lost my dad to suicide,
a choice he made.

i dwell on the thought,
wondering if he regretted the decision
he made as he was dying.

i ruminate what he looked like in his final
moments.

i am getting older
and he
is still the same age.

the day he died,
he left his bags at the front door.

addressed to me and my brother.
baggage left behind for your children to clean
and sort.

i untied the bags and was met with
an assortment of issues.

this is the baggage that lives inside of us,
because we are you
and you are we.

i often think about what my dad would have
looked like
with wrinkles and grey hair.

nostalgia, it's my history.

i'm crying because the roads you once drove on
are changing.

i'm crying because the grocery store you once
shopped at has been renovated.

i'm crying because the football oval we used to
spend time at together doesn't exist anymore.

you could say i am too nostalgic.

does sting know
that the sound of his voice
singing the songs of the police
makes me cry.
every single time
i listen to the music.

i can't swallow the lump in my throat.

i'm glad you get to be with your dad.
don't take him for granted,
you don't know what it's like.
don't be a prick to him.
he loves you.

i wish i could see my dad
but he's in heaven.
i never took him for granted,
i was just naïve.

grief is the final stage of love.

we had our good and bad times,
you raised me well, that's not a lie.

how am i meant to heal from this grief?

no man will ever love me like my father.
no man will ever do anything for me like my
father would.

rest in peace.

to the future, i thought i would have.

i still believe that you will walk through that door.

i pour my heart into tears,
never to be fully formed again.

why when i speak of my father
there is a pause.
an awkward silence?

it's okay,
humans pass away all the time.

the change of subject emerges
but he still lingers in the air.

they don't know how to react
when i say that my dad is dead.
"was he sick?" they ask,
"you could say so", i reply.
"was it cancer?"
"no, it was suicide".

the look of regret
immediately covers their face.
i laugh to make them feel comfortable,
"it's okay, you didn't know".

ruining relationships
looking for you.

this is what happens
when men don't heal.

i feel so bad for her,
she had no clue.

how could god do this?

but

did god do this?

he beat god at his own game,
taking death into his own hands.
so who is to be blamed?

god?
or my dad?

emotional scars,
i try and try to heal.
why can't i?

maybe i should seek help,
but i won't.

i never want to be unsad
about my dad passing away.

i believe that the pain i feel is proof
that he was real.

our love,
our relationship,
was real.

i don't want to reach the point where i don't
at least tear up
because then it lets people know that i am okay
with him being gone.

i will never be okay with that.

be grateful for your suffering
as it allows you to empathise
with the suffering of others.

my teenage trauma is all about you.

are you trying to get through to me?

try harder.

i cannot hear you.
i cannot see you.
i cannot smell you.
i cannot talk to you.
i cannot touch you.

why am i embarrassed to ask questions about my dad?

i wish they would just tell me stories about him.

how many of my little quirks belong to him?
how much am i like my father?

no one can break my heart
as badly as you did.

i was a couple of months away
from having that real teenage connection
with my dad.

i'm starting to realise that my parents are human too.

would i be this sad and angry if he was
accidentally killed?

life asks a lot of me,
life asks a lot of you.

always presenting problems constantly.

learning from our lessons consistently.

life asks a lot of me,
life asks a lot of you.

death.
the demise we are all faced with.
i seem to have accepted my fate.
but seem to not be able to accept
the fate of death
for others.

i am half of you.

i was so naïve,

i didn't realise my dad was abusing substances.
i thought he was acting normal
and one day he just
switched.

that's what terrified me the most.

i thought he hated us
but he hated himself.

fragments of my soul left me
when you left this plane.

starved of life,
starved of love,
starved of connection,
starved of you.

i'll never look into your eyes.
ever.
again.

the fact that he no longer walks on this earth
was the first thought that made my tummy drop.
many years later,
this still makes my tummy sink
deep into the ground.

i just want a hug from my dad.
am i asking for too much?

you apologised to me before you left.
you knew.
you knew.
you knew.

you knew you were going to ruin your life.

forever suffering in your pain.
trying to heal what you left behind.

there's been a lingering pain in my chest.

i gaze down,
i notice my heart has been
stabbed,
slashed,
and sliced

into a million pieces.

i cannot fathom actuality.

who will walk me down the aisle?

some children have no idea
what it is like to have a good relationship with
their father,
so they imagine it.

i know what it was like
and now it has reached extinction.
never to return.

maybe i hate you,
maybe i don't.

i could say you ruined my life,
but i am not a victim.

mum said i wasn't allowed to be.
mum said i have to be strong,
i have to be masculine to survive.

i'm not someone with a victim complex,
i'm just someone who craves the past.

when i look up at the sky,
whether it's cloudy,
blue,
or starry.
i hope you're there, looking down on me.

i didn't get to say goodbye,
no final words.

you stopped protecting me on earth.
protect me from heaven.

a flower started to bloom in your presence,
holding your finest essence.
a flower started to wither in your absence,
falling into obsolescence.

i hope he's surrounded
by angels and eternal love,
that's all he needed.

i was living
blissfully unaware
that you did not want to live.

our last moments,
i did not know were our final moments.
but you,
you knew.

i am so angry with the actions you took
and i don't know how to express my anger.
you taught me to keep it inside, to stop sulking.
so now i cry alone
in the comfort of my own company.

i want this pain to be over,
but when it is over,
does that mean that i will never
cry for you again?

i am so afraid of losing my grief.

i miss you more than my heart can handle.

you live through me.

my favourite chocolate bar
is yours.
my favourite tv show
is yours.
my favourite music
is yours.
my favourite soft drink
is yours.

addiction takes over
when your childhood needs
are not met.

it's not fair
to see others happy
with their dad
when that should've been us.

i can't run away from these feelings anymore.
they live inside me.

they say you need to feel to heal.
i'm feeling
but i don't think i'm healing.

heal your childhood wounds or you might commit suicide.

heal your mummy issues or you'll become an addict.

heal your daddy issues or you'll develop depression.

how could this be happening
to me?

it's hard to relate to anyone with my grief,
my situation is so specific.

i could not enter the depths
of your darkness,

no one could.

you were long gone
under the surface.
stuck in the deep end
tied to a ball and chain.

never
again.

i don't know my paternal generational history.
who am i?

a huge wave of nostalgia
swallows me
when i realise
that i will never be the same
and neither will my life.

stories of my father are becoming just that.
stories.

i wish to leave this place
and not grieve for anyone.

your life could turn
in a matter of a second,
for it to never be the same again.

but what are we without change?
even if it is the most devastating.

you were so capable of love.

you were so capable of spoiling it.

when did you learn
how to tie the knot?

there is no one to protect me
like a father does.
i feel anxious and alone.

A letter to dad 29/10/2015

i've been wondering what you're doing. i miss
you and i miss your cups of tea. for me,
schooling is going well and dancing is still my
thing… wish you were here. i'll always cherish
our time together. when i feel down, i can
remember you called me darling and that makes
me feel you're near. one day when i'm eating
home-made pizza and watching your fav show
seinfeld, i'll shed a tear, but have no fear… cos i
forgive you. I LOVE U.

it's bittersweet,
i get so overwhelmed in nostalgia
being in my hometown.
i'm sad because things have changed.

don't forget to turn the lights off when you leave a room.

that's the last thing i remember my dad teaching me.

you cannot force someone to change.
you cannot force someone to be better.
you cannot force someone to seek help
you cannot force someone to feel loved.

it's such a shame that we die.

where is your astral body?
i want to find you.

you sacrificed this family
due to unresolved trauma.

now i feel it is my mission to repair
but these are not my wounds.

time
flies
by.

am i embarrassed that my dad is a murderer?

you're always in my memory and i'll take those
with me.
unfortunately,
i'm starting to not remember.

your death wasn't inevitable.

i dream of a future with you in it.
a broken dream,
that never really got the chance to start.

i long for the summer sunday mornings,
the sweet scent of freshly mowed lawn
filling the air.
the gentle breeze kissing my skin
as i peddle my bike
down the familiar streets i'm growing up on.

i feel like i no longer know who my brother is
anymore.
because of what you did to him.
his consciousness left the planet
the same day you did.
i cannot lose him too.

how do i know
that i won't be a bad mother
to a daughter who will have her father's love,
a love that i no longer have?
how do i prevent my jealousy of a husband
who showers our daughter with his love,
when that love is all i lack.

you had a family
and you still left.

the physical time between us
increases.

the spiritual time between us
decreases.

i struggle to live in the present
because you don't have a residence there.

you're alive in the past.
i would rather be with you.

life was easier then,
no worries,
just a child.

everything happens for a reason.
what was the reason?

where did all the love go?

i guess if this didn't happen to me
i'd be living a nuclear life.
my character wouldn't be so developed.
i guess that's something to be grateful for.

i'm always ready to
expect the unexpected.
you just
never know.

jealous of their love.

you failed to see the beauty in this earth.

i don't blame you,

but we all have our ordeals.

my dad wasn't strong enough.
the devil snatched his soul.

i don't blame him.

my brain gets foggy
when i walk down the streets
i used to roam.

every tear that escapes me
makes up for the heartbeats
you'll never have.

whatever my dad was battling
was bigger than him.

my father,
my dear father,
what happened to you?

in your youth,
did something happen?

in your adolescence,
did something happen?

in your adulthood,
did something happen?

my father,
my ill-fated father,
what happened to you?

you killed your family
and you killed yourself.

i want my man to dance with me
because my dad used to.

he missed his kids.
he bought us presents for every birthday and
holiday he missed.

it was quite surreal to realise
that he really knew me and my brother.

but he knew twelve-year-old me.
i was fifteen when i opened those presents.

i laid eyes on the girl i used to be
and the girl my dad knew.

she ceases to exist,
she only existed in his memory of me.

i cry for who i used to be.
i cry for who i will become
without you.

i'm wistful of my past.
i struggle to look into the future
because it is hard to grow from this.

my brain is tired
from thinking about you
every single day.

you must've been in a horrible place
for your only option to be suicide.

i'll get a random urge to start crying,
they'll ask me what's wrong.

i hate giving the same answer.

one less person singing happy birthday to me.

we know nothing lasts forever,
but you were meant to.

nothing's the same,
everything has changed.

perhaps
i should see a medium
so i can talk to you.

this grief is different from the others.
i don't believe it will get easier.

just know that life is everchanging.
there is no beginning, middle or end.
not the way you imagine it.
but just know that whatever you're going
through,
you are not alone.

oh my goodness,
how different my life would've been.

you can't heal the pain
you refuse to feel.

i sob at the moment
i truly understood
and became aware
at the realisation
that is the first time my parents
are going through life too
and they can only do the best
with what they knew.

sorry to all the people i know who lost someone close in their life.
i'm so sorry i don't know how to make you feel better.

everybody dies.

not afraid to die anymore
because you'll be waiting.

i'm sure of it.

your life is not the same
once a parent dies.

they say you cannot plan for the future.

you can plan for your death.

that's precisely what you did.
more than once.

nobody tells you
that when someone close to you dies,
it'll be a bright sunny day,
you'll be driving down the street
and for no reason at all,
out of nowhere,
tears will start to well in your eyes.

your mind takes you back to that trauma
and you feel it all over again.

look after me, please.

Resilience

i was driving to the sting concert for work,
it was raining, i got a flat tyre.

i screamed to my dad in the sky above,
"why don't you look after me
on the other side?!"

and then it hit me.

the biggest lesson my dad ever taught me
was how to be resilient.

i'm always so emotional when i think of you.

it's annoying,
because i'm always reminded of you.

i struggle with not feeling good enough.

being your daughter was not enough
for you to continue living.

to know that i can't call you on the telephone
and ask how you're doing distresses me.

why am i in so much pain?

i could break every bone in my body
and your loss would still hurt me more.

if love could have saved you,
you would've lived forever.

you will be brought back here to try again.

good luck.

i seek the masculine father archetype
in my relationships.

dance with me,
treat me like a princess,
teach me new things,
protect me,
be my first love,
because i lost mine.

i'm homesick for a home
that i no longer belong to.

i think about each life milestone
and how you won't be there
to celebrate with me.
birthdays, holidays, graduations, dance concerts,
leaving home, my first job, getting my driver's
license, my wedding, the birth of your
grandchildren...

won't i be happy?

will i be able to celebrate with pure happiness?
i genuinely do not know.

sometimes we don't want to heal
because the pain we feel
is the last link
to the love that we've lost.

i am a new person; a woman.
my dad will never know this version
of me.

now i dance alone
in my kitchen.

you used to be there.
dancing with me,
singing along.

a duet turned solo performance.

the people i meet,
he will never know.
they will never know.

he died many years ago now,

so why do i catch myself thinking
about what my life will be like
when he magically becomes alive again?

i miss my dad, no one seems to understand.
literally no one.
i can't talk to my sibling about this, or my
friends, or my family,
everyone experienced his death differently.
even my friends who have a deceased parent
can't understand.
every grief is different.
no one i know experienced a great healthy
relationship with their dad,
who one day changed and became a scary
monster,
instilling fear into everyone and suddenly ended
his life.

my life feels disoriented.

who are these people?
that know who i am
without my dad.

my five-year-old inner child is confused and in disbelief.

my eight-year-old inner child is devastatingly heartbroken.

my fourteen-year-old inner child is burning with anger and sadness.

my sixteen-year-old inner child is lost and disappointed.

my eighteen-year-old inner child is afraid.

you've torn my heart into a million pieces
and taken some with you.

will they ever return
and make my heart full again?

how can i be frustrated with myself?

i was only 13,
i was motionless.

the devastation of his loss is indescribable.

if you combined every emotive word
that described a negative feeling,
that is how i would describe grief.

when he visits in my dreams
i try to make the most of it.
yet it's the same story,
he's always saying goodbye.

daddy issues,
father wounds,
i am no longer the same
without you.
you broke me
into a million pieces.
you gave me grief
without a reason.

i hope to see you in the flesh one day.

years on,
hindsight teaches me
that nothing i could have done
would have changed anything at all.

i can't smile at the future.
the knowing that you will not be present
aches in my heart
until it's my turn
to disappear.

my tears are holy and mending.
the only way out is through.

i know i need to dedicate more healing for
myself.

i'm starting to understand you,
a little more.

the battles you faced,
a little more.

the hard drugs you did,
a little more.

the self-destruction,
a little more.

the choice of suicide,
a little more.

i wish for you to appear
into physical form
from the abyss
and say hello.

there is no comfort to this grief
is there?

visiting the house,
we all once used to live in.
memories i'll cherish forever
with my dad, my mum and my brother,
my friends, my grandparents and others.

i must say goodbye and let go.
attachment is the root of all suffering.

my inner child feels lonely,
she's asking me not to leave her.
therefore, i must not change.

hold me safe, hold me tight,
for only you see the tears i cry at night.

how i miss and long for you
you were just a moment passing through.

i think about you every day,
not a moment goes by where i wish you had
stayed.

i pray i see you in my dreams,
but even they are bittersweet.

now all i have are memories,
i hold them safe and tight within me.

acceptance
slowly but surely comes.
denial
is still very present.

To my brother

i'm sorry. i hope you heal from what we went through.
you were my first best friend, i am always here for you.
i love you deeply.

there is courage in my pain.

time is passing so quickly,
i wish i could rewind.

it turns out this isn't the first time he's
abandoned me.
he did it in a past life,
or two.

why do you continue to break our contract?
what did i ever do to you?

nostalgic for something
that never happened.

To my mother

i am sorry my father put you through this.
your strength continues to amaze me every day.
thank you for everything you did to protect your
children.
i love you deeply.

it never occurred to me
when you were crazy
that i would end up spending my life
missing you.
i had just never thought of this outcome.
i see you in my dreams
but it's always the same story.
i feel you in the music you used to listen to.
and yet,
somehow,
you're not here.
how bizarre that it is my imagination
that continues to keep you alive
when you were once physical.
i could look away and you'd be gone.
i miss you
and i do not know
what to do anymore.

there is no time limit on grief.

A note on suicide

to inflict pain on yourself
is to inflict the same pain on others.
the rope that hung you
kills your family too.

don't be selfish,
think before you act.

suicide is not the solution.

enoue'ment.

i will try my best to not be like you,
to not let go of my life,
to hold on to myself and others.

i will try my best to be just like you,
you brought me up to be this way.
i am grateful for that.

will it ever go away?
i'm afraid it never will.

my ego is trying to understand suicide.
i need to intellectualise, rationalise and make
sense of it all.

except i have more questions than answers.

my ego's grip on trying to understand
is slipping through my fingers
because this is not something you can rationalise
or intellectualise.

i continue to have more questions than answers.

my ego stopped trying to control the meaning
and understanding of suicide.

i think i am free.

i saw you in my dream,

you don't speak to me.

but we lock eyes,

and i know,
and you know,

this is it.

i love you to the moon and back.

AUTHOR'S NOTE

Thank you for choosing to read my story. I have poured my heart and soul into these pages for almost ten years. My dad passed away on the 15th of July 2015 - I was 14 years old. My father ended his life on his terms, and it has taken me years to be able to proceed on my healing journey. It was very difficult for me to accept that this was my life and that my dad was a closeted substance abuser. I remember being happy and carefree in my childhood. My parents raised me well. I was 12 when my parents announced their divorce. I was surprised because I never heard them fight once. Not long after, my dad started to disappear slowly, and for almost two years, my dad was acting in a way that I could not comprehend at the time. Suddenly, it seemed, on a Thursday afternoon, my mum told me to take the next day of school off. I was suspicious, but it never even crossed my mind that I was missing school because my dad was dead. She told me and my brother the following day and that changed my life forever. The healing journey has not been easy and I believe it will never end. My heart goes out to everyone who has suffered from grief, whether it was your relative or your pet. It is not an easy journey and hurts either way. As you may have noticed, this book has a Part One. Part Two is more uplifting, as I have been made aware that the healing we do within us affects the deceased's healing within them.

I see the light, and I am walking towards it.

www.ingramcontent.com/pod-product-compliance
Lightning Source LLC
Chambersburg PA
CBHW021353090426
42742CB00009B/844